EVERY TONGUE CONFESS

Every Tongue Confess

David Craig

RESOURCE *Publications* • Eugene, Oregon

Resource Publications
An Imprint of Wipf and Stock Publishers
199 W. 8th Ave., Suite 3
Eugene, OR 97401

www.wipfandstock.com

PAPERBACK ISBN: 978-1-5326-6825-8
HARDCOVER ISBN: 978-1-5326-6826-5
EBOOK ISBN: 978-1-5326-6827-2

Manufactured in the U.S.A.   11/09/18

Contents

A Father's Heart

Abraham had no time for the future, the "river of faces":
mighty kings, fools who would bear an imprint of his mind.
(Gifts behind a current he wasn't permitted to see!)

He noticed the light flicker inside his distant tent.
Let all goat-hair be God's! Let the night trees move
His song. What can a servant do but follow?

He imagined his past, people ill-used, shorted:
"Let every enemy I've made be blessed, double;
let me be broken enough to give them ear."

Who is this generous: the Hand that carves the plains!
Himself, he was nothing, a gatherer of sheep, a man
alone, without instruction—a man without place.

What could he give but the cooling night in the ground,
the ways of animals? Perhaps it was his common
ways that marked him: the snore, the open-mouthed nap?

His heart was not a father's heart today.
It was a leafy passage, the waking of smooth stones.
He would be a desert welcome: for animals, men.

Jerez and the Siege of Vienna

Why is it, if we had no religion, Muslim, we might
be friends? Yet God is too good to leave us alone.
Gates open, jeweled, one hand finds another.

People have come before; they knew how to speak.
They lived in the quiet, fed on loss. Ask them
their names, and they would offer the rolling sea.

Saints part the heavens with the plow of earthy voices.
The rest of us wait until we get a nod.
Take my hand, almost friend. We will save each other.

Only they can count, the holy ones. We are more soil,
the wind through barren factories, a night of wet branches.
(They are like lightnings, ranging out over the ocean.)

My family lives here. We are small as most in this town,
live where others have: in the creases, with our lawns, mowers,
our attempted gardens. We know sweat and the price of wine.

If you moved next door perhaps we could venture a cheesecake.
Our children are older now, but we have rakes.
Our God has not left us here without the means.

Miriam's Only Candle

The hand that shielded, that held the baby close,
the moon and the plagues hidden in dark water:
things are always worked out right in front of us.

What's good always starts out small, somebody's irritation—
and then soldiers are dead, piled like municipal cordwood.
(They're easy to move out of the next greater way.)

The least of us move about like favored sheep,
God, a high fence against an insistent wind.
(Did you think the righteous would share their food with you?)

The smallest stones are what we own, our name,
no one's concern. (Who deserves more than that?)
That's where we run along the fence, my friend.

But the stars shine brightest here, boldness has play.
Jesus's name is a tent that flaps forever.
Write your name with Keats, on the shifting waters.

The night barks. The stars will be your only company.
He will shield you from the edges of rain, a life
so small that no one can ever take it from you.

Where the Dead Stay Dead

Twenty-three thousand casualties are never enough.
We need to die with the brave! We need to wash
the lean-to until it becomes something altogether new.

War never solves anything. It opens wounds
that were never meant to close. It's an Amherst window
that looks out with Emily Dickinson, taking in the rain.

It's a wooden version, from 1862, with just
a sometimes screen. We had no defenses back then.
Babies fell out of second story windows.

A mother's grief owned most of this finite space.
Sweat was a constant in summer; hair oiled your head.
The country around you asked for more of the dead.

It's why beauty sold like hotcakes. It offered respite.
We live where no life remains, among the dead
at Shiloh, each odor, a stain, reaching up

from the moil, bloody leaves. In our hope we are birds
singing over the bloated bodies, the snapped plants.
It's a dark tunnel, where the dead stay wounded, dead.

When my Wife and I became One

we hadn't. Not yet. We were like young farmers in the field.
We were much less than older hands would make us.
We were the cloth, uncut; we were wild roses.

But the birds always showed up then! Every morning they sang
and woke the grass. Any fool could've heard the noise—
and we did. It's her age, beauty, that attracts me now.

The wisdom, wit, in a life cut of its own wood,
one that offers nothing outside itself; the presence
of God is a field of onions, her bed's smell in the morning.

You could bake with this woman, nod as she plays her Bach.
The house could fall down around her and still she'd close
its doors. (She's made the place, brick by brick.)

It took awhile for her to learn grey. But it came
naturally, like women learn everything. When she's on,
you know why you are here. You forget the rest.

The world runs past us here on the farm; pig's ears
perk as night settles in. Let it take what's left.
We've our dotage, plants, a hundred balls of string.

Monet's Beads

The haystacks undid him so often. They were unrelenting,
especially during sunrises. A cold answer to streaks
of pink. Another world, forming its flesh.

In the end, he had to give up straw like morning.
He'd leave them behind. Skylarks would help, shooting up.
The ground was just that, where you started from.

The rest of the day was the print after the foot was gone.
A place of mercy, for children; a place he could live.
If there was a God, this had to be Him, he knew that.

We come here to inhabit the mystery of our lives;
we come to touch God's invisible face, with our paints,
our hands, until He rustles in every room.

This was how Monet would paint, getting his lines,
colors from some other side. He'd wait until
the waiting finally found its place, just disappeared.

He couldn't name creation, but the holy prayer
made him every day: his call, the answer.
Let the monks have their beads, cells. He would wake the world.

A Second's Bow

Death called Gabby Hayes, anxious about the routine
she is always being asked to provide: just another
sidekick: duende, always the joke, the gern.

Who wouldn't be grumpy, "persnickety"; who'd have time
for these "young whippersnappers"? They eat your beans,
take the siesta spot closest to the fading fire.

Though she doesn't bring anyone into this happy world,
she's there for the ride. She makes us human, adds contour,
grace. She makes tasks matter, creates suspense.

She gives us the form of the play: the final door
which isn't one. She's only solid in the run-up, a prop,
closeted at the end of another working day.

Would it be too much to give her her due, a shout?
She's craftsman, a rose each soul can wear in its buttonhole.
("Consarnit" is all Doctor Hayes can finally say.)

Teach us to dance with our "Sister"—emissaries, footmen,
as she pushes to break every heart in the final room.
I ask for an eye to see how she finishes this play.

St. Eudalia and the Barcelona Variations

Barely finished with her childhood games, she would rove,
studying toads, clutters of spiders. Then she'd wait.
When she was finished, was she happily so?

Tuesdays make demands enough for us; weakness,
thy name doesn't matter. Today it's mallets, croquet.
We live on the downtown plain, riding its streets.

We wait for the same old bus, no matter its number.
This is how heaven ferries its fools, in a trail of exhaust.
We make our weak attempts to improve ourselves.

No one gathers to applaud. (How is that so!)
This is how Jesus finds us: sitting on curbs,
abstractly thumbing through books that offer life.

You know our names, our schtick: Alphonse, Gaston,
(our faces, as long as Cortez's, the Panama Canal.)
Since we can't draw Him down, it appears we have to wait.

Who would have thought our faith would come to this?
A running self-conscious commentary—"Biking for life."
God is like a moon, in the distant quiet He walks.

The Lords of Misprision

It is a big city, where we live. You can't find a taxi.
Pipes get broken. Steam issues from the street like bad
intent: it's a thrumming bass line, what's left of your life.

Which is why basketball makes so much sense;
order is tentative here, a momentary effusion
which is more of a last-days promise than anything else.

That's why Marvel invented superheroes. It's why kids
still play on the street; they catch the fire, are happy
to let it go at the end of the day. "Carry peace

in a private bag," people say. "One on your left side,
one on your right." Let them affect your walk,
the way you call your distracted friends. It's jazz

that omits no man, or woman, no feathered dispatch.
Charlie Parker! Now there was a real Catholic!
I saw him once in K.C., in the farthest back pew.

He was always playing his horn, even when he wasn't.
I know he had Jesus there, on his sacred tongue,
because I could hear Him dancing—on hot afternoons.

Losing my Incompleteness

It's like that pocket hole, your pens sliding through—
the spaces designed between your dexterous fingers.
(It's as if we didn't really belong on earth.)

Maybe that's why we take treks across the globe,
why the sun keeps disappearing. Reminders everywhere:
old friends, how they wither right in front of us!

Even gloves wear out; the holes for my buttons fray.
I would drink to your health, but I don't want to press my luck.
The next day will come, and I'll have to find a new ear.

What is created is gobbled up, is tasted, found good—
and wanting! Transience makes the planted flag snap;
the newest chicken lay a bigger, more colorful egg.

We dance so we don't have to remember. Death gave birth
to rock 'n roll. And recess. Remember that.
(The jitts came later, after the march of the happy mushrooms.)

That is why I sing the way I do: Praise Jesus
for my incompleteness. I don't know what today will bring,
only that it will come in buckets! We'll form a line!

The Potato's Prophetic Eye

Our door plaques speak us: we are the venerable placeholders.
Even our clothes, hurrying with a fray here, a snag there;
they seem almost anxious to find a new home—Goodwill!

This is where wanting never stops, where nothing is ours.
Some call it holy poverty, others, money's start.
(Either way, there's no help at this particular table.)

What are we, friends, but leaves and the sun breaking through?
Facts say we are solids, but those books are way out of date.
What are we but the speech of heaven, beyond our sin?

Even this blather, what is it but a sprinkling of God?
He allows us participation: we name what we cannot stay.
(We can call this one: "Going by, Very Fast.")

Jesus is raiment on the lake: He speaks in movement,
has allotted us days, these beautiful, fleeting rooms.
What can we do but sing in the heaven He gives?

My "alleluia" is a step on a summer sidewalk,
my daughter's latest i-phone dilemma: beyond me!
Let us count our blessings—on what might be fingers.

The Strangeness of Summer Trees

Friend, grown men are often strange. Take Plato—
please, the hooligans who tried to pass as his friends.
How many philosophers can you count on, and to do what?

Take my plumber while you're at it. He's lost a whole person:
two hundred pounds, but all he wants to talk about
is STAR TREK (my phasers, ears, long buried in the closet).

He has army men on his bureau; stones like the henge,
a large backyard circle to re-watch each series.
What could I add to the alien starlit proceedings?

It's because I'm so full of error, I think, can't speak
his way. Why does everyone want you to be like them
or some third party they think they already know?

I come from the Scottish paleolithic, a clan
which cannot come to grips with the most basic problems.
It took us three and a half years to select an ombudsman:

a tree with brightest arms, a healthy reserve.
We wait, move with him, delight in His wind, shadows.
It's odd, how we can be happiest when we're most alone.

Stealing Third Base

It was a grand bit of chicanery. Missed by those
too timid for the graced line of crime—no sense
of preparation, the technique involved. We had it, a gift.

Some of us kept the clippings, most what we could
of the ride. But when the horses went lame, we were left
on a dusty road—we had to change our names.

The same thing happens most times we open our mouths.
Before you know it, we're filing our nails, painfully
abstracted from the lives we just can't help but share.

Sign language could help us to temper our verve,
(or we could insist on a commerce of Anglo-Saxon,
though that wouldn't bring back Beowulf, the honest beot.)

We could reduce our expectations, of course, get lambs
to gambol, maybe hawk some aperitifs—refraissant.
(We might get a papal blessing, buy a frame!)

We dance with the only person we ever bring,
dress him up as best we can. He can puppet with the best.
(Don't let his wink fool you. He is a prisoner of desire!)

We Thin Up, Blow Away

—for the Jack Attack

My next door neighbor gets older quickly, thin hams,
hair going its older spare way; he can't claim the moment.
(So much of him has left for Paris already.)

He shows courage, knows how he is seen, trying
to hold on, in the boots, shorts, with the spade next
to the younger backhoe guy who is digging up his yard.

There's a great virtue in being less. It's how
we are, yes, but we get to teach the world
as well: what it knows but never chooses to see—

that each of us is Parkinson's fare, a spring-green flame,
a modest light. Like the cloak of distant stars!
(Each with a promise it cannot deliver: our companions.)

Shorts and boots is as good an answer as we
can expect: a small city lawn and the yawn of a worker,
everyone in his place on this neighborhood yellow school bus.

Our lives play out right here, without fanfare or counsel,
in a smattering of summer noises, a swimming pool
somewhere, an adolescent guard barking orders.

The Love Poems of Calderón

are stuffing the poor box. They speak to the ribbed vaults,
buttresses. I bet a few have translucent wings:
saints' fare. But poets have never fooled anyone, Pedro.

We know that you drink alone, near the halls of the dead,
scratching out poems to some secret love who'd waited
too long among the damask curtains, dark lace.

All of Spain lives there with you, or did, before
she ate herself. Back when every Spaniard was Black,
his posture, fine. Now poets look like everyone else.

But this isn't about what's left: the cardboard houses,
the politician's face. It's about what we expect.
(I strike a match against a palace cannon.)

Nothing is ever as it should be. That's why we invent:
all of history, Yeats at Toner's, literary pub crawls.
You could say we feed on the white of lilies, on lies.

We invent approximate loves. "These will have to do."
But only the sorrow lasts. It makes us go out
after love again, until we become every need.

Some Real Growth

My daughter named her first four dolls Margaret,
home schooled each one. They baby talk in Latin.
I have no idea whom to believe anymore!

We all sin like there's no tomorrow. Unspectacular
from the start. Maybe if Walmart had a facelift department,
I could focus on my pervasive lack of trust.

(We'd pitch pennies behind the grade school steps,
having cut Mass at ten to smoke our cigarettes—
my dad's stogies, curing at least one of my sins.)

Wasn't there supposed to be some growth by now?
Wasn't I supposed to turn into somebody else?
How many years will it take to complete this turn?

We open our mouths to try out our first long vowels,
embarrassing anyone who's paying the least bit of attention.
And today is still the diner where everyone starts!

Sporting an insect antenna headband, Jesus
walks us. Today He's a great lover of melittology.
(We're among friends here: this is how we proceed.)

The Mailman Works for too Many People

—for Br. Daniel Klimek, TOR

He passes by, modest, skimming the roses;
but who knows intent, his secret agent's heart?
(On Wednesday nights I bet he bowls with his mates.)

There's life here as well, like in those Italian movies:
Romantic, with pasta, wine, the winning smiles;
bright cutlery set out on sunny vineyard tables.

Our suns come up, in rain that speaks to the birds.
We all twitter like summer does when its branches bob.
We make friends with every bug, bright blade of grass.

Even on the bad days, though our lives can quail;
the impossible saints we've tried to copy protect us.
Mercy sends us what we need, wrapped in pastrami.

This Die-er, Riser. He waits as bloody Truth.
We beg out loud to make ourselves less than we seem.
The Middle Ages claim us as we locate His body:

the glistening sweat, because we can't bear the gore.
It's a place in time where each human must go alone—
His cooling skin, its ripeness: like some kind of fruit.

Dancing with Denver, Colorado

I hitched, didn't know with whom! The Bohemian guy
who wrote lyrics, liner notes, for The Spiders from France?
The guy who rented me second story rooms in Tremont?

I met a version of him later in Chicago, outside
a museum, reading his poems to no one but the wind,
violent edges of pages, a night lake in the background.

The silence, like the rest of our lives, spoke in the clouds.
Women didn't seem to frequent those alleys—back then.
The boymen, lost in a haze of alcohol, on benches.

Hope was nowhere around. Or so it seemed,
though the Greyhound Bus Station had a passable cafeteria:
crust of mashed potatoes, a promise of places.

Things haven't changed much, at least when I do the cooking.
Our cars usually run, though we're all on borrowed time.
It's good that other places still live inside us.

A purer poverty there, in the food we can afford,
slightly mismatched chairs, patched paint on the walls.
My wife is the moon that guides this ship through town.

Having a Son is too Great a Burden

Your choicest parts have already embraced your wife.
The rest is chicken feed, you fanning his life
with answers he currently is unable or unwilling to hear.

You are a cask of cellar wine, Van Gogh's wind
blowing across empty portions of northern France.
Your son reminds you of this when he starts his car.

Who can measure the breadth of his sorrow? Who can speak
the courage of men who have come before: the great
reserve, "The Order of the Tarnished Spear"?

This is why fathers and sons don't speak very often.
They each row a silent boat, oar-locks for one.
(This is why they always keep their tools so clean.)

Women don't know what to make of these brusk silences,
of the words formed in dark places (other-worldly tool
and die), set against a life men didn't make.

This ends with you taking down your son's picture from the mantle.
You keep repeating the scene—until you can't.
And you understand something about Abraham's knife, cross.

Nikos Kazantzakis and the Donkeys of West Virginia

They could have names of the early friars: Leo,
Cuthbert, with their ample middles, their matted coats.
They search the Holy Writ of grass for their next move.

So generous, who among us would not have joined their rank?
I'd wear a small wooden assbone around my neck.
I'd speak loudly, hold out for some real change.

But they are the arm you un-nail, too, the one
that flops over your shoulder as the head lolls.
(All the donkeys follow for miles in an ancient line.)

"Now, brother, it's your turn," Jesus might say, as you clump
down a path, crop some green. You might be Nikos,
a child, running through Greece, not knowing your name.

Or in Freiburg, at the end of things. It would not matter.
Your friends would call you until you couldn't hear;
then the others would start, the ones that guided you.

Donkeys through the donkey door, as it's always been.
"Nikos, Nikos," they shout. Like the hills that bore you,
like the town that still speaks your mother's name.

The True Wife

If she is patient then she will wait for you.
She'll come in a Walmart sun, with a yellow slurpy.
You'll be sitting on a dusty road, in the wrong place.

Love is never kind when you start out, my Friend.
We learn the way only because we have no choice.
(We would just as soon eat pickles in the pouring rain.)

Angels do what they can, mill about as they wait.
"Tell me, what's going on today, little brother?
Will you re-invent another kind of third wheel?"

Little brother never listens. That's his ornery way.
He says, "Let God come through here," and of course, He does.
(It's a very old trick in that first book of His.)

He says, "David, grate me some cheese," robe settling
around him as he sits. Then we hear the kitchen noise,
Jesus, eyes closed, humming the Da of the universe.

That's the last thing you see: two odd ones in the dirt,
waiting for the wife. She'll be drawn by this (or the cheese).
Where she is is another happy story.

The Scorners Outside Us

They expected us to be better people. To queue up for a ball—
to have read the damned book! They really don't ask for much,
after all, just the sun, rain, some purple clover.

But I can never make my tie come straight, and that's
just the first stanza. The next thing is the car I drive,
my side of the road. (And Keats was too poor, too short.)

This is what it means to wake up in the morning any more.
It's the white noise that gets us out the door,
the piazza in Florence, Dante's mask, his font.

The Etruscans had the same problem, except for them,
it was small red flowers. They came out everywhere, along
foundations, in the living room. Foreigners laughed.

But everything is praise. Much that is, all that will be.
And the road doesn't finish. The blue sky is not king.
It is a glorious stepstool. That's why we write these poems.

The world is a flag, waving us as we wave it.
(Make sure no one falls off!) Jesus does make laws,
but only for Etruscans who are so slow of heart.

Fifty Scholars Typing

—for JS

It's a big basement. The bustling quakes our hollyhocks.
Our chickens get nervous. And who can blame the hedge?
It feels, like Shakespeare, as if its height's been taken?

And it's not as if we don't deserve some trimming.
Something's got to keep the monkeys up at night.
Who else will bang on the blasted typewriter keys?

Besides, safe passage is never helpful here.
Whatever comes will be a gift we have not deserved.
Which is why we gather like toadstools after heavy rain.

Our scholarly friends feed us beneath the caps.
It's how we know our bodies, the companion earth.
(Take half of this for granted, the rest on faith!)

So we, too, get tested, repent if we think we know.
Flowers open every day, which is a kind of hope.
The Mass book too. (Linda greets me every morning.)

What else is there to know? On some days life
is all there is; it ripples through the biggest flowers.
All the typing is a sound we just might want to hear.

Living in a Stone House

Your hand hardens as you reach for the granite door.
The place absorbs sound, squats, a gift from the Mesozoic.
It wants to move beyond the lies, the self-service.

Here pressure creates, it's the thing's need to sing.
It wants to find the furnace. It's the heat it seeks.
It wants to dissolve into purer liquid form.

Granite knuckles, your voice seeks its deeper shaft.
You share a rage with everything metamorphic.
(Posings won't take you where you want to go.)

Dust gathers on you as you wait! It's all you can do,
standing next to exploding window glass,
waiting to be set free from frames, from the illusion.

It won't help, of course. Stone nights don't make us new.
It's the violence we need, until our rough surfaces
give the night a better name, begin to change.

We will be a stone bell that won't ring out the night;
we'll advise the planets, offering the only way.
We want to break the compass of ample thought.

The Earth Finally Opens Her Doors

I don't know why we weren't invited earlier.
We could've brought along a few meat trays,
banana liqueurs. I could've been emeritus by now.

But life's always like that, isn't it: first the Mayflower,
then the rest. And really, who can argue with timing?
We're happy just to have a lounge chair seat,

a penny spot for the applause, the apocalypse.
Order of arrival won't count for so much then.
Those without names will wait for the expected call.

The groundlings will respond on cue; there will be hoots,
some back-slapping. The popcorn will pop itself.
I want to see what Humphrey Bogart will say.

Then, the only climax we will ever know,
when the time to kid one's self has passed, when the fields
thin, when you have to stand next to what you've done.

Jokes will end. And you'll be happy to quiet
in a soup line. If you own patches, they might help.
We'll see we've been playing someone else's game.

Friends and the Big Vein on the Back of Your Hand

Friends are like porches, the buckling of old tongue and grooves.
They are like dark roads that pay their own winter tolls,
or a worker who fashions iron points in a gothic church.

Who of us is up to the task of hammering all day,
hauling gargoyles? The village drew straws and you lost:
guardian of the pew, old school practice, police.

All the vegetables are local here; the meat is lean.
The Mass burns in everyone. It's where they live.
No one steps out of his place. God rings the bells.

And soon enough we see angels lighting on roofs;
they offer their wings, food to beggars on cathedral steps.
Blossoms float everywhere in a sunny weekday breeze.

No one asks why you are smiling. They have their missions.
The weather, too, is perfect for these mythical times,
as chaffy workers troop home from alfalfa fields.

Each one is happy to see his family, little Stevie
and Beth. You do not live here, but you could.
All you'd need would be a book and a pair of glasses.

The Kiss of Jesus

has turned the water that runs through you into wine.
The water table is now your friend. You can coax
pears out of trees, get coupons from the grocery store.

Given that, you'd have thought that everything would turn
out right. It would be like the end of a previous life,
each silver step as it was truly meant to be.

This never changes. Ships may come in, go out
again. The seasons will change just to remind you—
what you have does not end here. It, specifically, endures.

Did you think that you were loved before? Did you think
you knew the sparkle, glint, of His doting eye?
Welcome to the laughter, friend, to the stony road.

He who loves you in earnest has taken you to Himself.
He is risen in your body, because that is what He does.
It's in the catechism, first page to the hokey last.

He has a name, and He shall be called "Answer."
And you shall dance like sunlight in the grouted squares,
in the patchy arbors, His kiss upon your mouth.

Robert, You Know how these French Poems can End

Friend, the river changes your life, every time.
You fall in love with the bends. And then you expand,
paint in little blue circles, write anything you want.

You will no longer live there, amid the cup, saucers.
You will be an unsettling influence, like Françoise Hardy.
God Himself will have your full attention.

Nothing will ever be the same, though that's how
it's always been: you get up, your clothes have been moved,
all your friends have disappeared. You wish them well.

This is why you're here to begin with, why you have
so many turns. Each day is a joyful caw,
the keys on the piano, the notes, the fruitful ellipses.

That is why we do this. We love rustling papers in the wind.
We love to speak our Lord's unfinished word:
we move our mouths; I call Linda or after the dog.

We call. We call. We call. This is our delight.
It's not like an answer. It's as close as we can come.
Let that be the happy French song* we sing today.

*"Le Large" (on YouTube)

The Leper Gets a Job at the Apothecary

All of us, walking down from the hills, together, in silence.
It's cinematic: a twig snapping; next, a close-up
of lined faces. We are children of the morning's chill.

We came here seeking our home, where the stones can shout.
We will break with an opening in the trees, feel leaves again.
There will be something to stand for: a quiet, expressed.

This is who we've chosen to be. A voice who forms us:
birds, they will have a new resonance we can't pin down.
It might even give us new letters, an alphabet that matters.

We will slowly begin to root; coins at our feet.
They will be our laughter, their shine on foreign faces.
(It's our joy that will find the others, new houses there.)

We will bask in an almost native reserve, hum some.
We will be like lovers, holding hands with the twilight!
Our sound will shake the clouds, all the trees at night.

This is what it means to open among the living:
to be the tree the blind man has learned to see.
God spits, and a thousand new farms crack their seeds.

Magdalene, her Heart went Everywhere

She wanted to be a person no one could become,
every turn promising glitter, a better name.
And after each party it covered her, wet streets.

When He came she felt like grass before the sunrise,
like a grey morning of floating geese, the water.
He saw right through her, past her tawdry show;

He warmed His hands at her broken hearth, told her
morning comes, like the smell of early pine!
The Father's days are like does in a misty break.

So her rooms became smaller, her life, hidden within.
She talked less, had less to say. She walked behind.
And as was fitting, He took no notice of her.

Until the day He did. And then, His fire
met Itself in the dark corners of her broken heart.
(His hands, touch, would've been the Father's throne.)

She did what we all do: she oiled His feet.
She waited to be of some use, happy not
to matter much. Everything had order again.

The Inflatable Backyard Pool

We are saved, but only for as long as we are not.
Like pink flamingoes, we rest, silent, on one leg,
beaks down—on our feet. The journey must lead the way.

Or not, He's not talking—except over morning water.
Who can fly before the moment we wait for comes?
Which of us can right a time that hasn't arrived?

Trees and garlic help us with our daily bread.
Our friends, neighbors, have more goodness than we can believe.
(What would I give now for a life of laying down track?)

We live in an opened paradise, though we can't know
what any of it means. This is why people invented
tobacco rolls, returnable soda pop bottles.

We can jump up and down. Nothing changes for us.
It's like we don't even get to vote on the subject.
I wish someone would tell me where I can lodge a complaint.

It's like Jesus got real busy all of a sudden.
Or maybe He's still trying to make His first point.
Either way, salvation is always just out of reach.

The Brood of the Morning Dove

But joy doesn't have time or place for any of that.
It's creating whole other rooms, breakfast nooks.
Come with me, friend; I'll show you my shotgun, my stump.

We can call on St. Francis, hear him speak old Italian.
Some manic kind of preaching by the unquiet pond—
but then he'll calm, pull up a meadow seat.

St. Anthony brings bread to rip, gestures to the sun.
He's hardier—a rout—more than I would have expected.
(When I move in the stiff wind, I become a tree.)

Then Jesus is at it again, rioting the woods!
It's like He just can't make Himself at home.
(It's true, you can't dress Him, take Anywhere anywhere.)

This is why I can live the way I do, erratic
praises, my books, my out-of-season clothing.
(Rightness is all, as Shakespeare might have said.)

The world is our ballroom, friend, each step made to free
it up. But then, of course, we'll have to leave.
What did you expect? We can't stay here forever.

I Know Nothing about the Lesser Antilles

Mists can teach the skin, but who knows what?
Wet ferns, too, undo me, in garden or in forest.
I remember where I live—but not how! Why pretend?

We lift our feet high because we don't know where we're going.
Our buttons misalign. We should walk around that way.
We should smile widely every chance the world gives us.

We always miss where life is, the confusion it needs.
That's where the dance is pure. That's where we serve.
(So much offered in a steaming plate of pancakes!)

Jesus says His name slowly. It's the friendly eye
of a garage, in everything we've forgotten to do today,
on colder nights, when the apples close themselves off.

He was there that night when my neighbor died to be
with God. I still don't see Jim every once in awhile,
which serves to remind: we're playing this game for keeps.

Everything is a surprise when you think about it, the drive
from my alley to the road is never the same: a rabbit,
willow branches trailing new ways up my windshield.

The French are Genial, which Makes a Lot of Sense

Thérèse is French, and proudly so. Her flag
made her happy. Aquinas loved his books.
It was the architecture there that made his home.

Both could talk for hours about the little things
they loved. And you will be happy to take it in:
the houses of God, much larger than you could share.

Yet they will not feel alarmed. You are there, after all,
another surprising gift—that won't stop giving.
The places you meet and make will be shouts of joy.

I might see one of them this Tuesday, noon.
Or you. (If you don't count the sins, we're the same:
duffers with brand new clubs—which is part of heaven.)

They are sporadic yellings in the field, a glossolalia
of children. Over-sized people in bumper cars.
More picnic tables than you'd have thought possible.

The plaza is always open. I want to ask
the Little Flower, what can I learn from the French?
She'll throw her arm around me, take me for a walk.

Ypres, 1916

It's a good thing death only lasts for a short time.
I remember what it was like in the dark that first time:
pre-natal voices promising others, a world.

Our time here is so short, so much of it behind!
Still, the shout is upon us. What's left matters!
Let me put on my boots, walk below the tree line.

Let us make our dent in what passes for civilization.
All these old Fords, muttering down the street,
no one with any idea on how to get home.

Books helped us fit in from the start (the world played ball).
There were typewriters back then, phones took our nervous calls.
It wasn't real, of course, just as this could never be.

What is actual took its time with us, still does:
everything you never got for Christmas, your birthday.
It's third grade, made right this time because it was.

Will the battlefield look like this after we're dead?
Will small seedlings grow in our palms—find root there?
Will that be the only time we ever see it right?

The Adriatic's Blue Coast

It's the places you always go to when you're alone:
a farmer's market where the fruit is a little too small,
a ripe pear at the grocery, the Croatian sunlight.

The only world is the one that makes you, inside.
It gives the rivers form, the stars a sky.
It's the pool you find there, that has named your reflected face.

Where else are we going to live? Where heaven meets
a better earth, where sky-y willows touch water?
This is what we have to give to the next person we meet!

Jesus! Who do you think stopped and formed all of this?
Twigs of wrong reason resist the cataract, but to no
avail: the noise is joy's price, it's summery date.

He called and you answered under a green canape.
That Eden is always enough, though it doesn't live here.
So you are fog feet, with no coastal place to rest.

Everyone wants to dip their toes into the Adriatic
before they get there, to give more than they can.
How else can they be open, move out of the way?

Baal Shem Tov and his Slide Rule

Each hand has five fingers, more or less. I've counted.
You could say that fact is the ruin of us here below,
but that would be like closing a window to keep out the breeze.

Scientists dance among the elephants in their rooms.
So many! Many without names or places to sit.
(The pillows of importance, that's what matters here.)

Philosophers help them with the counting; after all
that's what good neighbors do. It's a busy hive.
A fit place for man and beast, angels and pages.

No one goes where he's not needed. The lake can always
use a viewing. We go to what is next on the list.
Someone named John is always there to meet you.

You squat by the prone man, your car, hand him a tool.
He tells you his vacation is coming up pretty soon,
and you're happy for the Outer Banks in Northern Carolina.

If your life were a prayer this dance would be much easier.
You could sit with Bacon around the empirical fire,
stroll with Baal Shem through his fountains, sparkling rooms.

The Planets Take their Time in Pronouncing Vowels

We stand, either among the forgiven or the forgotten—
smudged. We're God's and pleased to be tatters, bells.
(We'll give you place, since we have none!). Forgive me,

and I'm like a dancer coming finally alive.
I begin to remember the steps, the rooms, the faces.
But isn't this every day of our burgeoning lives?

How else could we ever hear Jesus? His big moon face,
the story of the night trees; I could listen forever,
Him frying up some Cajon fare on the stove.

The world is always opening up before us.
It's everything we've never seen. Who could ask for more:
the planets, rotating, each keeping its own counsel?

Name me everything, Lord. I will gape like a fish.
My time goes by me here, but my name does not.
We can finish as we tend, over there, among new trees!

I say alleluia with them, my arms and hands,
the busy sounds of forgetfulness. My wife could come too,
my fishbowl, a few hasty papers beneath my arm.

Across the Waters of a Blue Grotto

—for Dr. Lynn Divis

It's the other pearl of great price, the high-water mark.
We're forever paddling across the flood in our tubs.
On the whole we've seen far too much of us pass, Friend!

As we age, our colleagues, one by one, take leave
of these hollow halls. Each absence takes consolation with it.
(The academic gong has always had a hollow sound.)

Younger people are, again, taking over the world,
though they surely won't be able to fix it either!
The whole project, a bit of a sham from the beginning.

Like us, they will give their years to what is passing,
this lovely place of ruin that has watched, conspired,
made us root and grow, wither when the time came for that.

It's been friends in buildings, students and colleagues both.
Now a copier sits upon a Capri precipice somewhere,
chugging above a Blue Grotto, its work never finished!

What you have given now belongs, for a moment, to others.
And then we will be part, again, of the stream—as we've been:
in painted tubs, turning, singing harmonies.

The Alhambra is the Sound that Bears It

Like our lives, a palimpsest of sin and glory,
or the Spanish wars, its ancient hymnal—architecture.
In the end it's the King who matters, who speaks this brocade.

We hope for lives that come clean, the insides of the cup.
May our praises bless the night time, with tambourine;
may we live in the basalt, clay, that spell us here.

Let the earth's discontent, deep ruptures indict, name us.
May our sins march at our sides, fall into our graves.
There will be no escape. What we have done, we have done.

We're the notes that bind heaven to swarming gnats.
And we've not nearly finished paying for our needs.
This is why the saints sit near us, bear different names!

How else can Jesus make the world itself again?
It is blessed by souls, by feet who've known the lies.
There is no religion that does not take us here.

And that is why we always look ahead.
To the One who will come, Who already has; He speaks
and seedlings find a million ways to get it wrong.

Rembrandt's Unruly Monkeys

The stars never stop failing, falling from the sky;
there are props in this play: trapdoors, floating capes.
Choose anything, try it on. It might even help.

Were you that child too, standing, without family, cut off
in the lonely sear and noise of a field, among grasshoppers?
Did you wonder why you felt so yellow, like them?

You'd gotten no letter. Had no companions for this trek.
My parents said they were so. We were offered a future—
nothing. No one is equipped to survive this world.

The next steps eluded me, though I walked through the days,
as everyone did. Adults came, offered activities:
a breadth necessary to set me to a mysterious task.

An eye slowly opened inside, as disappointments mounted.
There was a pond within me, a place to settle, see.
Only God could've offered this other-worldly quiet.

And then the joy finally came, with His better name.
Jesus brought wings, the start and end of things.
He offered a foreign way—the exact same field.

The Only Cardinal at Antietam

It's telling the soaked world about the dead,
giving them burial, among the blackened trees.
This, Friend, is what we get for living here.

Well, what else do we know? Singing birds, the cost
of friendship. Let's sit down among our failures,
swords and fine ancient rifles in our keeping.

Fictions and not, history will not help.
What swords we have have trained us for nothing. We
will be tested here, and we will fall again.

This is what it means to stand up and exercise.
This is what it means to make a point, to insist.
(It's a good thing we do not run this show.)

And so we sit in the valley with singing birds,
toeing the broken toys in front of us, knowing
that what is futile cannot be changed by us.

Greatness does not live here. It never has.
We get up, shake our packs, our canteens (off the cold).
We won't be defined by the proofs we have gathered here.

Another Century Spells Defeat

Not that this statement comes as any big surprise.
Each country sets the rules for its own demise.
So we wait for Basho, walking sticks in the country.

Jesus sings here, in the clotted leaves, gutters.
Millipedes are His dearest friends. You might think He's too busy
cranking out legs, a thousand dance crazes;

but no, He's up rattling wooden shingles at night,
calls us by our Confirmation names. We have only to listen,
and our ignorance quietly sets a darkened table.

We stand on the porch, listen to sheets of rain.
The tractor gleams under a light (where Bill
and I played a soaked, drunk game of garage basketball.)

We wait like we always seem to, in Your absent Presence.
Jesus, feel free to tap along any wall.
We cry out again. Make us new, align.

Let the laughter we share tonight redeem our farm.
We'll line up our shoes for you, kneel next to our children.
There is no way to make any of this fit (in Iowa).

The Soul is in Love with the Nightly Movement of Snails

Souls long for a mouth much closer to the wet meal of earth.
I know for certain that we do not live in this house.
That's why we invented windows, doilies, book shelves.

Snails, on the other hand, do not live in discord.
They have accepted the ground's invitation. Bound as one,
the two of them bob like dark waves of the Baltic sea.

We have our angers, they rise like Indian mountains,
pushing the Himalayas around like a kid in gym class.
(We invented glasses in the fifties, just to knock them off.)

The world, repentant, calls us back to marshy ground.
Deep places know: to curse anything is to misname it.
Let us live in the forest, where painted faces can settle.

Jesus, these moments rise up and crack wet tombs.
No one rises this time. Just the awakening grass blades after rain.
Houses hunker in a web of clotheslines, nightly distress.

You're the gravity which comes to settle these squealing nails;
the cold world is held in place for another day.
We are bucking horses, tied to rails in a sunny field!

Augustine

He is not alone in this. The flag on his ship,
he knows, is as futile as every plan he's made.
He tries to enjoy his watch, does so every night.

It's like when he, as a boy, carried walnuts uphill
in his shirt. How else could things ever be? All that's sure
is that he will have little say in what happens today.

He is central to nothing—when he's close to the center of things,
a Center who takes us through the only moment there is,
though the past never seems to stay where it belongs.

Jesus, these days, seems a modest island westerly.
Augustine wonders how long can this lull last?
(The speed of the troughs seems to define each storm.)

So his struggle is to stay alert as Jesus prays—
though no apostle walks here. His sins live in the steeps
of a deadly sea, in the straining of seasoned wood.

But God's always willing to start smaller, which is a good thing!
It's how much of us He can find. Rhetoric, intent—
high seas within seas: a Rose which fashions simplicity.

Separation

It is true. It's all we know. Even when words,
for that briefest of moments, suggest the larger thing.
(The world, after waiting this long, locking into place!)

It's your blue drape, the sky, a baptism had,
a sacrament in the deepest part of a swimming hole.
It's the praise that's due, a praise that doesn't come from here.

Nothing is yet, of course. There are a thousand races to run,
all those new faces to see. (A disappointment or two.)
And Mary, patient as only a mother could be.

Stillness owns the sound it lives for: the shout
from heaven, the joy we are happy to be a part of.
We stand around, an answer we've got to give.

Let it be an innocent rolling-pin sound from the kitchen,
the early spring in a morning mattress: to task!
Whatever it will be, let it be too small to notice.

Jesus, doing that, doing all the rest as well.
We are faces on the road, lost among roadside flowers.
Each will turn its face, draw us together again!

The Empty Space We Reach for

It must come first, the void that answers our prayers.
Death, in spangles, can come next, dancing, alone—
while a party goes on in some muffled adjoining room.

She might take you by the hand, walk you down a hall.
You'll realize that this could be a Swedish film.
(The media is full of places you'd rather not visit.)

That only thing you can bring to field is yourself.
Why else do you think that you were invited to this shindig?
You wait a long time for the bonfire, some new strangers.

(Nothing surrounds your papery pearl shell. You flake
even as you sit. It's a kind of new white world.
Every party you go to ends up, somehow, here.)

It's your soul you always wind up talking about.
That's why the Father invented, invites, all these people.
As real as you, they come, in long white-face.

And so life comes down again to the strangest things:
that gun guy, when you hitched the turnpike for a tow
one Christmas, or waited for Mary at Garabandal.

Mandela and other Sorrows

There's a surfeit, a glut, of the sweetest things: "necklaces,"
ghosts at Nagasaki still prowling what might be coasts.
(We kill while pulling milk off the grocer's shelf.)

It would be nice to have something better to report,
a "very good" next to "plays well with others."
But that would be no one any of us really knows.

Mankind is a tree scratching at the fallen sky.
(Churchill is still fire-bombing civilians somewhere.)
Only God can take the scope, the horror, in.

Our quiet is never enough. Our repentance can seem
thin. But death has been warmed over too often
to be a mistake. We live by the snows of repentance.

So the good always happens, like clover, on a little road,
way too early in the morning. A gardener waiting
to tell you what no sane person would ever believe.

He carries a locket with all the faces intact.
"Wait here a little longer," he says—disappears.
You kick at a rock, not really surprised—again.

Meeting at Night

We meet ourselves at every turn: in waters,
dark ricks, where no Browning, no kin, can ever reach.
A marsh puts every night in its proper place.

England never lived there either. She's a spot of silver
on the island heights, the sun's surest friend, confidant.
She will die along with the rest of her colony: Europe.

We grew up alone, and nothing here can save us.
Can you throw up your hands if no one is there to see you?
Can you be someone new when the old won't give place?

Only the guilty rise. Only they never change.
It's the oldest dance there is: the sin we move in.
The silt heard it form the hearts of druid princes.

It beat that helmet, Sutton Hoo, into shape,
though metal craft didn't help much then either.
Each person must walk this dark road alone.

It's important to know that you cannot save yourself,
that you had nothing to do with putting you here.
You are an imprint, waiting again for the Hand.

A Poustinikki

—Catherine Doherty

Li Po would've poled the river to visit her cabin,
St. Francis supine, singing, in the moonlit boat,
a vale of crickets pointing out the way he knew.

We are left with vestiges—a way we cannot take.
This is the saints' gift, a future you cannot have!
It's a way station, a place to walk a lake.

And honestly, how much is there to work with here?
A few scraps, perhaps, some wind, writing on water,
Shelley's effusions, spoken in a Protestant cemetery.

We're small candles, shielded from a broken wind.
We live in a world of our betters. Our only hope
is in time that stretches ahead, that it has its reasons.

There's a vastness in each minute, a cropping too large
for speech, that still, like Augustine, might pluck us out.
(God's plan is so outrageous anyway. It's possible.)

We'll sit with Peter, Francis. Think about that.
What kind of God is this? And they won't mind.
Heck, they might even walk over, pull up a chair.

"Doubling the Madness"

Which is, of course, no madness at all. Let's face facts:
it's a fish we'll never catch, an Odin song.
It's the we, the end we so desperately want to be.

We dabble where we never live. Sing our tree bevers,
our comings and goings—stories for an Irish pub.
There's a reason why Tolkien invented hobbit holes.

Bly's songs give rise to our own as we take to our hills
and rills, our halfling burdens, cutting everything
down to size. Lift a stein to a smaller world.

The great is for the great, after all. We get what's left.
We carry our stan, lift what we still can.
(If we make it to second breakfast that will be a success.)

In another life we could have been a dentist.
Nice little home, berries and many children.
We could have joined the Rotary, played golf drunk.

It's better to lie down with loss, to know what we can't.
Besides, there's a lot more burrow room this way—
we live for our lives, for what is achingly familiar.

Cézanne's Second Wife

Her name was Aime. She knew Montana's rolling plains,
rode horses bareback, a yellow rose in her teeth.
She was quiet as the morning, except on high feast days.

I don't know about you, but things never go my way.
My teeth could all be fixed, and still the bird
of not-here would come and perch on my left shoulder.

What do you say when people seem to dis-allow you?
What do you do when silence, like a friend, smiles back?
(You can grunt in peace as you work toward the heart of things!)

Cézanne knew his paints, nothing else would come.
Mont Sainte-Victoire could've been the cleaning woman.
France could have danced a block over, in a different color.

The present wore him until he learned to move
in its sleeves. Answers, questions, they went the way
of evenings. A crust of bread and then some wine.

He and his wife seldom had to speak. They were part
of the voice of the time, the art that had to come.
Cézanne was happy all through his life with that.

If You can't Find Heaven

It will adjust its address. How do you think this poem
found you? Do you think they just appear on the page?
No, they are a holy rain, releasing the green.

You have come here for a reason. So you can bless,
give more life to the proceedings! The invented continues
to create the world that has given rise to it.

The whole town sits around the fire at night.
A world repaired is coming, people you could favor.
We are not fools, have come to make that so.

Ah, it's a beautiful orange pencil that draws us here.
It's a sky that has long been opened for its business.
We put our coins down, near the crowded fountain.

Don't tell me you've forgotten Rome, the ceiling, beaded,
in Keats's death room? We're where we're at when heaven
comes. We open a door, give up who we are.

This is how we go through what passes for our lives, isn't it?
"See what I'm not. I'm already somewhere else."
Maybe next to you, confronting an array of flowers.

Every Sitar Invents

an us we want—and the bain that has prevented us
from getting there. Each road we build travels
alone, wide enough for an Eastern cowboy's sway.

We live in that place, within our beautiful shell,
a place no other can touch, though we each must try,
with a God who can feel like sunlight, a soft green moss.

This is why we delight in walking along the beach.
This is why we have so few friends, even as the world
loads up on the grain it creates. Both things happen.

The music gives us a divided heart, its strings.
Something much larger has measured us for a fitting.
We wait, in the healing, in the sunlit sound of a creek.

How does one give back? Our hands are small, limited—
our span—over before we can adequately reply,
before we can rise up and fully meet ourselves.

The student waits, sitting on the pile of his life.
The next move is never his. Happy idiot,
what wouldn't he give for a day in Your heavenly court!

The Pope's Longing

He longs for dogs, having the run of the place.
He longs for the white mountains of his childhood, his nurse
who used to call him by a thousand other names.

Sometimes when he sips his coffee, he longs for the stark,
pocked and ravaged moon high above the pampas,
for the woman at the newsstand, her gritty takes on the neighborhood.

The darkness falling over Rome cannot save him.
John the Twenty-Third still walks night halls.
A Titian cries with eleven Apostles in the basement.

The lightbulb clicks on, and he washes his hands yet again.
The echo of a door knob turning is only that.
Jesus will have to save this day as well.

Flamingoes rise up as one in some tropical place.
In another, a bomb explodes, even as a fine
briefcase snap shut, someone whispers on his right.

He struggles to be small enough, to get out of the way,
as pigeons flutter the circle that's Peter's Square.
He will never understand the ways of God.

The Sarod Explores the Terrain

It knows the long-married, whose sins rise up and claim
what's left of the day. We own nothing but small things.
They're what we bring to Jesus, at the margins of days.

Nothing delights so much as a painted wagon,
the brush there in your hand. You lack the poppies
to fill it, but then wind moves through the tops of trees.

We could be living in a Hindu country. We could be
wearing wider hats. The price for participation,
penance, these strings, would be about the same.

How else did you think you would help; your errors pave
your spouse's way to heaven. Give thanks and proceed!
Bring her a crate of, or, better, oranges in a bowl.

What have you ever gotten right? You rise
anyway, because a new day is a new day,
and the Word, my friend, hasn't finished speaking yet.

Our hands rise up, filling fretless baskets with syllables.
Our ancient children tell us all we've missed!
We are like strangers, waiting for a foreign bus.

The Potato Bin

The sound of the creaking lid is a mother's song.
Who would have known such freedom was even possible?
And then, in time, we learned what we needed to say.

There's something so homey about potatoes, dug-up dirt.
It's why we can read Wordsworth on pallets at the lumberyard,
or race our grocery carts on Sunday afternoons.

The bins still speak of the old cabbage places,
of rooms and the smells we grew up in. This is why talk
about end times doesn't disturb us. We live down the street!

Our sins would surprise no one. And that's okay.
It is not our job on this earth to gather attention.
Which flower in the side garden outdoes the others?

It's best to live beneath all that, to cast
our lot with the green: a slow scooter ride in the country.
The world, its radio, is a life we don't have to live.

Jesus speaks, using the gravel, two worlds colluding
to create a live painting—where plant meets man.
Lord, take my ambition. Give it to the noise.

Bach's Mass in Death Minor

When it came to death, the old masters were seldom right.
It was too early. None of us are poor enough—
except perhaps Mozart. His Requiem shoveled him home.

Death, at any rate, brings us all to the same yellow field,
plays spades on a card table, moving from seat to seat.
Everyone waits for the guy to say something, anything.

A little kid, late-arriving, climbs a tree.
He asks about dominoes, and a crowd begins to gather.
Soon banners are erected, booths; jugglers appear.

Music finds its way. Differences are gone. It's like nothing
has happened: a sunny day in your last July.
You look at your hands and the transparency begins to fade.

What have you ever understood? Not the pews, the sunlight,
not the smiles of your dearly departed, their bad habits.
They were the only boat that could have gotten you here.

When it's early, and my grown daughter grabs a cookie,
I rejoice because I get to drive her to work.
These are pebbles, slow-bounding, in the holiest of streams.

Tobit's Climb (and Process)

It's tough to do when you're blind, but your son makes you whole.
And what's with the whole bird-dropping thing, the fish guts?
It's like Jesus must turn mud to spit to recover our eyes.

"Please cure me, and make me whole," you beg, over
and over—and most of you listens. But the other part
learns the value of the Jewish self, learns how to hold on.

Our place is always in flux, among angels. We know that,
so we pay attention to the Torah-like detail.
(It's the physical world that gives us the shape of heaven.)

St. Thérèse leads, shows me, again, her chin.
My daughter wants to know about this Tobit guy.
"Is he from West Virginia?" she wryly asks.

"Every time," I say, as we cross the morning Ohio.
This is the life of a pilgrim. We're ferrymen: the dead
to the living; the living, inventing lives, to the dead.

Let us be hollowed voices, waves, the lapping of God:
dark father, daughter. Let us be the fog horn, the vegetation
on the banks. The low and real face of the fog King.

Table Nineteen at the Criminal's Wedding

There's no call for our approval—our place offers only that.
We are not among the notable, the better dressed.
(Champagne spews from the mouth of a crystal crayfish.)

We have no gifts to offer the world. We lurk
among the uncounted. We receive the polite word,
part when the curtain makes its public demand.

We are grateful when the action moves us out of the way,
when we can get back to our lives, back to what's left:
mowing around daffodils, the local little league.

Life moves where life is, on the shady side of the street.
Our children grow, move into a younger world.
May they learn to bring it closer to our original home.

Only Jesus knows how the rest of this will play out.
He seems to have places for those of little use.
Hope was made specifically for people like us.

May our lives shower His in the doing. God knows we've left
a mess of the trellises, wonky with sagging string.
Look at the place as a cathedral of lilies: a plenty.

Notes

A Father's Heart

Thanks to Robert Cassidy for the title.

Miriam's Only Candle

The Keats line alludes to his epitaph.

A Second's Bow

Gabby Hayes was a famous sidekick in tv Westerns.

Duende is a heightened emotion, an awareness of death for Lorca, something that sleeps within the poet.

"Persnickety" and "Consarnit" were words Hayes made up. Perhaps he got them from having listened to the Bowery Boys movies.

St. Eudalia and the Barcelona Variations

The "Barcelona Variations," for a quick internet minute, was the title for some visual art.

The Lords of Misprision

Be-bop Charlie Parker was a master of the "feathered dispatch."

Losing my Incompleteness

The happy mushrooms are organic psychedelics.

Stealing Third Base

A "beot" is a straight forward Anglo-Saxon boast.

The Love Poems of Calderon

Toner's was reportedly the only bar in Dublin for Yeats.

Some Real Growth

Margaret is a popular homeschool name.

"Melittology" is the study of honey bees.

The Mailman Works for Too Many People

The poem is dedicated to Br. Klimek, whom I once heard give a marvelous lecture on meditative practice in the Middle Ages.

Dancing with Denver, Colorado

There were no "Spiders from France," though there should have been.

Tremont used to be a slightly seedy part of town on the South Side of Cleveland.

Nikos Kazantzakis and the Donkeys of West Virginia

Kazantzakis, oddly, died in Freiburg.

The True Wife

The Da in the second last stanza appears in Eliot's *The Waste Land*—and everywhere else (by all accounts).

Robert, You Know how these French Poems can End

One morning, fishing for something on the internet, I came across this wonderful song by Francoise Hardy. It seemed a little odd that I had never heard of her (since I really love singing poets). The movement of the song, "Le Large," found its way into this poem.

Rembrant's Unruly Monkeys

The floating cape comes from Dryden's "MacFlecknoe."

The Empty Space We Reach for

Once had the great fortune to visit Garabandal—a place of reported Marian visitations—to stand where St. Michael the Archangel had stood. (Cool.)

Mendela and other Sorrows

These "necklaces" were gasoline-filled tires tightly fit about prisoners' necks. They were then set on fire.

Meeting at Night

The "Sutton Hoo" is one of several 6th century English cemeteries. It has proven to be a storehouse of valuable artifacts.

The Browning poem is "Meeting at Night."

"Doubling the Madness"

This title is a variation on the last line of Robert Bly's "Listening": "double the madness."

If You can't Find Heaven

The Keats and Shelley museum at the Spanish Steps in Rome has mostly been restored. But the ceiling is the same as it was when Keats died there.

The Potato Bin

In poorer neighborhoods most everywhere, people habitually seem to steal shopping carts from grocery store chains.

Bach's Mass in Death Minor

The first line alludes to Auden's "about suffering the old masters were never wrong."

Tobit's Climb

Years ago, St. Thérèse showed up in a dream. She looked right at me, lifted up the shift of her habit and turned briskly away, saying: "I have done this" (thus the chin image). I've always taken that as a call to be stronger. (The jury's pretty far out there. But we can hope, no?)

Table Nineteen at the Criminal's Wedding

There was a movie not too long ago about "Table Nineteen." These were the afterthought guests who had been invited to the wedding (something patently obvious to those at that table).

www.ingramcontent.com/pod-product-compliance
Lightning Source LLC
Chambersburg PA
CBHW060159070426
42447CB00033B/2222